SELECTION FOR
FLUTE AND PIANO

THE OLD GUMBIE CAT
BUSTOPHER JONES   OLD DEUTERONOMY
SKIMBLESHANKS   MEMORY
MR MISTOFFELEES

MUSIC BY

ANDREW LLOYD WEBBER

ARRANGED BY DANIEL SCOTT

FABER MUSIC LTD
3 QUEEN SQUARE, LONDON WC1N 3AU

THE OLD GUMBIE CAT

2

ANDREW LLOYD WEBBER
arr. DANIEL SCOTT

Legato (Glenn Miller flavour) (♩ = 104)

BUSTOPHER JONES

ANDREW LLOYD WEBBER
arr. DANIEL SCOTT

OLD DEUTERONOMY

ANDREW LLOYD WEBBER
arr. DANIEL SCOTT

SKIMBLESHANKS

ANDREW LLOYD WEBBER
arr. DANIEL SCOTT

MEMORY

28 Mevd

ANDREW LLOYD WEBBER
arr. DANIEL SCOTT

MR MISTOFFELEES

ANDREW LLOYD WEBBER
arr. DANIEL SCOTT

Printed by
Halstan & Co. Ltd., Amersham, Bucks., England

SELECTION FOR
FLUTE AND PIANO

THE OLD GUMBIE CAT
BUSTOPHER JONES   OLD DEUTERONOMY
SKIMBLESHANKS   MEMORY
MR MISTOFFELEES

MUSIC BY

ANDREW LLOYD WEBBER

ARRANGED BY DANIEL SCOTT

FABER MUSIC LTD
3 QUEEN SQUARE, LONDON WC1N 3AU

THE OLD GUMBIE CAT

ANDREW LLOYD WEBBER
arr. DANIEL SCOTT

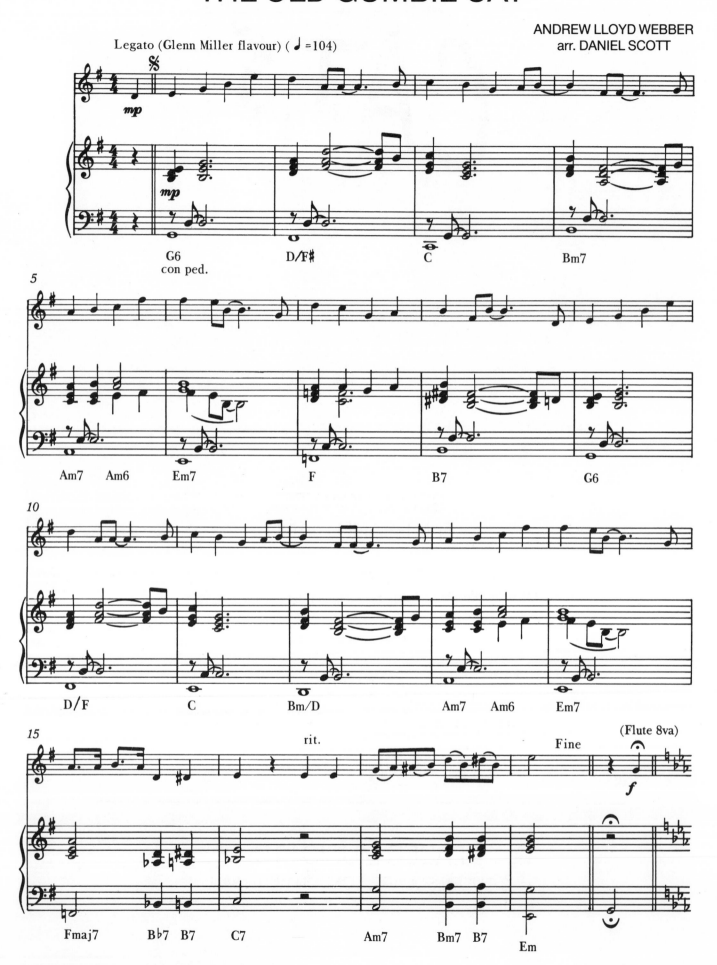

3

BUSTOPHER JONES

ANDREW LLOYD WEBBER
arr. DANIEL SCOTT

OLD DEUTERONOMY

ANDREW LLOYD WEBBER
arr. DANIEL SCOTT

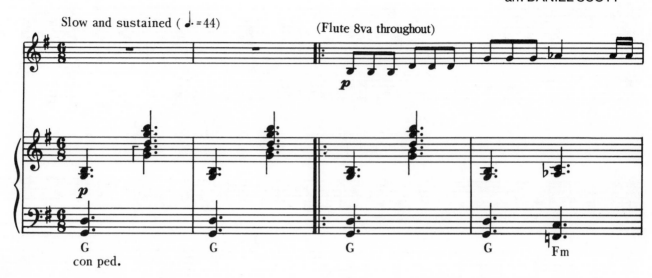

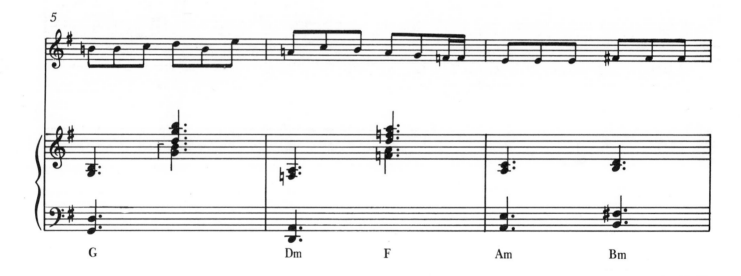

SKIMBLESHANKS

ANDREW LLOYD WEBBER
arr. DANIEL SCOTT

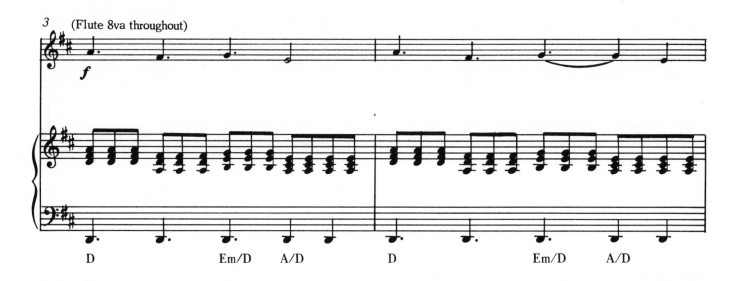

MEMORY

ANDREW LLOYD WEBBER
arr. DANIEL SCOTT

MR MISTOFFELEES

ANDREW LLOYD WEBBER
arr. DANIEL SCOTT

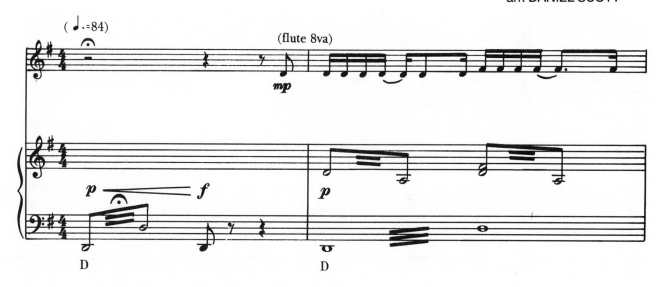

Printed by
Halstan & Co. Ltd., Amersham, Bucks., England